Rare
Earths

RARE EARTHS

POEMS BY
DEENA LINETT

FOREWORD BY
MOLLY PEACOCK

BOA Editions, Ltd. ❧ Rochester, NY ❧ 2001

Copyright © 2001 by Deena Linett
Foreword Copyright © 2001 by Molly Peacock

First Edition
01 02 03 04   7 6 5 4 3 2 1

Publications by BOA Editions, Ltd.—a not-for-profit corporation
under section 501 (c) (3) of the United States Internal Revenue Code—
are made possible with the assistance of grants from
the Literature Program of the New York State Council on the Arts,
the Literature Program of the National Endowment for the Arts,
the Sonia Raiziss Giop Charitable Foundation, The Halcyon Hill Foundation,
the Dorothy and Henry Hwang Foundation, the Witter Bynner Foundation for
Poetry, the Estate of E.M.K., as well as from the Mary S. Mulligan Charitable
Trust, the County of Monroe, NY, and from many individual supporters.

Cover Design: Lisa Mauro/Mauro Design
Typesetting: Richard Foerster
Manufacturing: McNaughton & Gunn, Lithographers
BOA Logo: Mirko

Library of Congress Cataloging-in-Publication Data

Linett, Deena, 1938-
    Rare earths : poems / by Deena Linett.
      p. cm. -- (New poets of America series ; vol. 22)
    ISBN 1–880238–99–3 (alk. paper)
      1. Saint Kilda (Scotland)--Poetry. I. Title. II. Series.

    PS3562.I514 R37 2001
    811'.54--dc21

                                                00-046825

BOA Editions, Ltd.
Steven Huff, Publisher
Richard Garth, Chair, Board of Directors
A. Poulin, Jr., President & Founder (1976–1996)
260 East Avenue
Rochester, NY 14604

www.boaeditions.org

NATIONAL
ENDOWMENT
FOR THE ARTS

State of the Arts

NYSCA

We are those to whom green hills have been offered
—Czeslaw Milosz

And to those who come after us: Amelia, Sophie

Contents

Foreword

In *Rare Earths*, poet Deena Linett creates a treasure hunt and delivers that treasure through the glints and hints of mysterious shards. Framed by a seductive apparatus of quirky scholars' notes, this book achieves an appealingly elaborate M. C. Escher-like two-part construction. First comes the subtle puzzle of Book I— "The St Kilda Manuscripts," with poems that ask us to believe that they were created throughout three centuries, using letters and notes collected under the aegis of an archaeological dig on the island of St. Kilda off Scotland. Then comes the surprise of Book II—"I Live past You," comprised of fluid, entirely contemporary poems written out of a contemporary woman's life by an anonymous poet who seems to have been present on this dig. She is "the American" who lives on after Mairi MacIntyre, the Scotswoman writer of much of the "manuscript" in Book I, has drowned.

Steeped in geographical atmosphere and narrative mystery, "The St Kilda Manuscripts" display "documents," usually letters, that create the eighteenth, nineteenth, and twentieth century island world from sea storms to pox epidemics, from romance to child-birth, from food to religion, all with the deep, contradictory senses of isolation and community that life removed from the mainland confers. They also include the story of the scholarly invasion of the island more than fifty years after it was evacuated, and the letters of architect Mairi MacIntyre, who has successfully petitioned to join the dig. On the island Mairi forms a friendship with "the American," an elusive poet who, even after MacIntyre's drowning, never steps forward to identify herself. We can only presume that she is the author of the poems in "I Live Past You," which take us to the present day, using present concerns—love affairs, a woman's daily life—and a related geography—the Florida coast and travel in Scotland—to mirror and shadow the motifs of islands and isolation, of passion and abandonment, of the crossroads of change at which individuals suddenly find themselves.

Despite the seriousness of its subjects, this book is delicious to read. If a subtle book of poems, daringly and deliberately con-structed, can be called a page-turner, then here it is. The pure enjoyment of unpacking *Rare Earth*'s mysteries, many of which defeat resolution, is as tantalizing a pleasure as reading a murder mystery. The reader finds fragments that trace a woman's friendships, her marriage, her family network, the trials of her family history in a windswept place of the sea, and attempts to string together events and relationships, making sense of it all. Making sense is part of Linett's sophisticated aesthetic here, and she is determined both to lay a groundwork and to refuse to fill it in. In the true spirit of archaeology, she operates layer by layer—and so, frustrated but tantalized, must we piece together what must have happened historically and what must be happening now, and none of it achieves the commonplace linearity any reader brought up on beginnings, middles, and ends would hope for. No, in the spirit of the dig, or of just plain digging, the rarities that are unearthed are related *and* unrelated, connecting but disconnecting. As readers we are left to create a skeleton out of bones we are not at all sure belong to the same ancient animal. Nor do we know even what the animal's shape could have been.

Part of the reason the elaborate nature of these connections works is that Linett comes to poetry from the novel—not the potboiler, but the literary, even the experimental, novel. Her fiction writer's skill underpins her poet's art. Thus, she introduces us to many characters, many voices, and to the intriguing fact that one of the voices—that of the central "character," our Scottish architect, determined to trace her family's roots on St. Kilda—also began writing poems in the voices of historical personages whom she made up. Linett thus fractures narration to get at individual lyric moments in a variety of personae, including Mairi herself, Alec (Mairi's husband), Mairi's mother, the voices of the clergymen which Mairi herself created, a student named Maggie, various anonymous writers, and the voices of women imagined and real from the eighteenth, nineteenth, and twentieth centuries on St. Kilda. Many of the islanders have the same names, so we, like Mairi, have to conjecture who her ancestors are. Are the nineteenth century St. Kilda women, Mary Rose and Anna Clare, as well as a woman called Alma Rose related to Mary Rose MacIntyre? The poems conjure up a quality of relatedness without the actual fact. It is a poetic reproduction of that old argument in fiction: which is truer, the factual or the emotional verity?

Linett frames all these voices with the commentary from the three scholars who are bent on making their reputation with the discovery of the St. Kilda manuscripts. Then, to top it all off, she slyly refers to sketches and doodles that have not been reproduced. As the three scholars say in their Introduction, "Lacunae are part of the pleasure and appeal of archaeology. Gaps leave room for mystery. . . ."

Book II would be a straightforwardly lyrical group of poems were it not for Book I. Instead, it postfigures what has happened by investigating a late-twentieth-century woman's thoughtful but charged life, presumably the existence of the missing American who won't come forward, despite the three scholars' advertisements in various journals. This "the American" writes in an Emily Dickensonian tradition—however, she hardly leads a reclusive, Dickensonian life. "Clay Figures" both lays out the anonymous poet's aesthetic and excites the inventive postfiguring in the second part of the poetic diptych Linett has constructed:

CLAY FIGURES

Now we know the people who made us
were merely children, afraid
we would find out how little
they were sure of, and like children
grown bored with their toys,
they have gone. We are the charms
they turned from and forgot;
if there were words to keep them
they've been lost. The wind picks up.
Hills and trees that have slowed it are removed.
This is what we've always known:
they'd go out after dinner and not come home,
leaving us alone like small clay dolls
on the vast plain of the world. Now the draft
before the wide dismissive sweep
that one day will wipe us all away
the way a child's hand clears off a tabletop.

This poem could almost have been written by the ghosts of the figures in Book I. Haven't the poets and archaeologists "made" them? "Clay Figures" evokes abandonment: just as the scholarly investigators left the island, the islanders themselves in 1930 abandoned their home and island-identity, leaving the "wind" to "pick up" in that storm-tossed placed. Yet the poem has its Book II context of being emotionally storm-tossed, abandoned by deceased loved ones. This is a poem written by the grown woman who understands the limitations of all relationships as well as the inevitable erasures enacted by time, "the wide dismissive sweep / that one day will wipe us all away / the way a child's hand clears off a tabletop." The image, as chilling as the physical chill of Book I, recalls how the island has been swept clear, the dead now merely "charms." The caprice of time, like the caprice of lovers, scholars, and the caprices of the body in general, funnels down into the image of "the small clay dolls" abandoned by the ones who left for dinner and never returned. Clay, when smashed, becomes shards, and shards are what the archaeologist and the poet pursue. It is from shards that we reconstruct the life of the past.

But shards are broken pieces, and Linett's poems are quite unbroken constructions. Their dexterity and complexity glitter like gemstones cut with facets to mirror one another, or what one might imagine to be the kaleidoscopic view from a many-lensed eye. It's worth noting that there is a hinge poem at the beginning of Book II, "August Morning," a scene on a beach with lifeguards on a rescue drill that the speaker mistakes for an actual rescue. Suddenly she recalls a memory from fifty years earlier: her own mother attempting to save a swimmer. Of course all of *Rare Earths* is about this very process of diving down and dragging up, or digging down and lifting up, whether it's merely practice, as the lifeguards prepare for the real thing, or a scholarly exercise. All rescues, Linett seems to say, are *attempts*. "You're supposed to concentrate on the rescue," she reminds us, not on what you're recovering or whether you will succeed. In the attempt is the success. And certainly *Rare Earths* is a dazzling example of that maxim.

Molly Peacock
New York City and London, Ontario

Book I

The St Kilda Manuscripts

The St Kilda Manuscripts:
Editors' Introduction and Commentary

Background

The poems before us were folded into Mairi MacIntyre's note-book which, along with other artefacts, clothing and books, was washed ashore in late September 1994. MacIntyre, an architect and member of the St Kilda Study Group, was drowned when on 30 August 1994 the *Sutherland*, ferrying eight members of the Group to the mainland, went down in a sudden squall three miles west of the Sound of Harris. The note-book, which contains professional architectural drawings, sketches and notes as well as records of dreams and other personal material, was wrapped in oilcloth and bound with strong twine, and thus survived.

MacIntyre, who lived and worked in Inverness, left a series of poem-documents which attempt to limn a women's history—if such a thing is possible—of St Kilda and the Western Isles from early times to the present. Though most of the material following was written by MacIntyre, some pages are made from copies of existing documents. As imagination led her forward, MacIntyre developed other ideas: on the poems which show migration from Norway to the North of the country, she has written, 'what fun! A group I'll call "Foundations"'. In assembling her chronicle, which we believe began as an entertainment during the long summer nights, MacIntyre had help from a visitor, an American she describes in poem-letters to her husband, telling him that 'the American' has tried to imagine the lives of 'silent Presby-tee*errr*-ians'—that is, the women on St Kilda (rendered as 'the American's' attempt to replicate the sounds of Highland Scots). In another (to her husband),

> . . . My friendly American has gone,
> but hopes to come again next year: the bonnie Sutherland
> took her and several others home . . . .[I f]ind myself
> imagining lives of those who first came here,
> a kind of counter or addition to the work she's done.

And have added—you shall see!—a group of clergymen. . . !

15

In her letter of application to Mr Iain Fraser, Coordinating Director of the St Kilda Study Groups, MacIntyre wrote that she wished to go to St Kilda to recover the life of her grandmother Barbara Rose. Caution must be advised, however, since so much of the material before us is fictive, and since Christian names are quite frequently repeated throughout Scotland, and on the Islands as well, which makes positive identification difficult. Because the provenance of the materials is in many places not clear, we have given titles to pieces where no title was provided.

Lacunae are part of the pleasure and appeal of archaeology. Gaps leave room for mystery, as the poet has said, and so we present these materials with the hope that they will contribute to an imaginative recreation of the past, and that, carried by other currents, they will find their way back to 'the American' or to someone who knows her.

We have sought 'the American' by many means, including posted queries at universities in the US and Canada, adverts in the *New York Review of Books* and other periodicals. We and other interested scholars have written to colleagues from North American universities who may have ideas about her identity. The search has been wide, but to date without resolution. (The St Kilda Study Group's own records were accidentally destroyed by computer error on 14 November 1994. Efforts to gather copies of those documents are ongoing.)

Method

We have transcribed, but not edited, the pages following. In effort at formal consistency we have occasionally titled them, but when our 'rage for order' conflicted with the colour and personality of the extant materials, we have permitted the pages to speak for themselves.

An additional word about authenticity: we believe that MacIntyre incautiously, even unwisely, brought originals of a few family documents to St Kilda. Her husband reports that they had discussed this, and that his wife, a woman of strong will, wanted to carry the originals for their talismanic qualities. *Barbara Rose: Her Book*, referred to in MacIntyre's letter to Mr Fraser, has been lost. MacIntyre's mother recalls her daughter finding some pages in a family attic, 'a sort of note-book tied up with tattered ribbon of a washed-out tea-colour.' MacIntyre's husband suggested she copy the old materials. As a consequence, some old material appears on contemporary paper in her clear and fluent hand. There are also photocopies of what are clearly library documents, and, we conclude, some are copies of older documents whose sources have not yet been determined. Since all would not have been poetic in form, it is likely that MacIntyre (or 'the American') changed the lineation as she copied them out. Finally, given the variety of materials in the notebook, none of which is properly signed, we determined that our task was primarily to order the materials we have.

It seems fair to suggest that the lyric poems we are calling 'Book II—I Live Past You'—are by the American. Her influence appears to have been considerable. Our colleagues have seen, even in MacIntyre's hand, occasional echoes of rhythms and word-choices of 'the American.'

We have been engaged in continuous consultation with a distinguished group of scholars by letter, telephone, e-mail and fax. The log of our consultations with them, and their comments, will be found in the Archives at The University of Edinburgh, which are composed of all materials referred to here as well as other letters, books, sketch-books and drawings, professional and whimsical. Some of the more personal materials remain under seal at MacIntyre's husband's request until 2074, after which they will be available to scholars.

We believe that the study of history is illumined by contemporary lives. Consequently, while we have not always agreed on the instant matters, we have all learned immensely from this labour, which has been one of profound pleasure for each of us despite, and even on account of, its complexity. With the caveat that the discovery of other materials will substantially alter our (temporary) conclusions, we finally determined to arrange the materials in a general chronology, with occasional departures from strict sequence. We hope the clarity to be gained from such organization will enhance readers' experience of the materials.

Information useful to overseas readers: St Kilda is a group of four islands in the North Atlantic 110 miles west of the mainland and about 55 miles west of Harris in the Outer Hebrides. The last remaining St Kildans were evacuated by the Government at their own behest on 29 August 1930.

We are grateful to Mr Iain Fraser, Mr William Boyd and Ms Margaret Adams for their contributions to this endeavour, and to Mary Rose MacIntyre, for permitting us to study her daughter's letters. We are grateful to Mairi MacIntyre's husband, whose family name does not appear on these pages in accord with his own wishes. MacIntyre was thirty-four at the time of her death.

Michael Alistair MacBain, Curator, Art Gallery and Museum, Kelvingrove, Glasgow, and Senior Lecturer, University of Glasgow

Sarah Ferguson-Gilbert, University of Aberdeen

Stephen Smith-Forester, University of Edinburgh

Mary Clare Writes from Uist, 1730

We have word of a bad time on Hirta.
You remember winter two years back
The year of the pox and storms.

With her husband my sister Mary Rose
Had seven children—two thrived.
One of those, my nephew Martin and his pa

And other men and boys were rowed
Out to Stac an Armin to take razorbills
And gannets, puffins and guillemots.

Then came the pox and laid low
All the men who could handle the boats.
They haven't got a proper harbor

So in stormy weather and in winter
They must take the boats out of the water.
The men were on the stac, or sick

The women as well, so no one
Could go out to bring them back.
Gales come fierce off the Atlantic.

I saw a map once, four years back.
It hasn't got her island or the stac.
Even fine cartography on vellum

Doesn't show the way the land falls
When you round a curve or how
White stone marks your way home

From the church under the moon.
They stayed the winter on that stac.
I think about that when I'm warm

By my fire, the wind and the waves
Grinding it to crumbs of stone
Beneath them and the wind going

Day and night. They tied the boys
To the men so they wouldn't blow
Into the ocean. Galey days songs

Argued with the wind and rain
And heartened them a bit. Then skies
Would clear but there was nothing

To eat, only birds and eggs, not a berry
Or a bit of green all the year long.
Sometimes they fancied sails.

It must have been hard to see
It was just the fog moving off
And not a body for miles. Next year

The boat came round to Hirta
And found so many had died,
And were told about the journey.

They went to pick them off that stac
And bring them home. Mary Rose
Says they decided then, her man

And the boys, to come to us at Uist.
I make her fruit pies, fancy lace
And suchlike. She takes a little interest

In the garden but they are not at home.
They miss the sea as it looks
When light pools on your own green voe

And the waves are still. They miss
Walking up the hill to the cairns
That mark the spot their bairns are buried.

You come to know the waves
From your own island. Now the boys fight.
The older cut his brother with a glass.

Mary Rose says she'd go back right
Enough but who knows how
They could live so far out now.

*I must have descended from these people—she
cares for 'fine cartography' and 'vellum'!—*

The note above is in MacIntyre's hand. The events are historically accurate. Hirta is the old Gaelic name for the largest island of the St Kilda group. A stac, sometimes skerry, is a rocky outcrop in the ocean. Voe comes—as do many place-names in the Highlands and Islands—from Old Norse, and means, in this instance, bay. The pox: Clothes sent from the mainland released year-old small-pox germs which sickened the islanders, causing many deaths and the great suffering recorded here. —Eds.

Unattributed Fragment (1)

—found beween the stones in a drywall on St Kilda, 1987

Tonight I fancy the moon's road over the water to Skye
Is firm enough to tread on, so I take it, stride right out
Upon it where it flattens near the rocks hard by.
Wrapped in oiled wool and my cloak, warm as an egg,
I step along the moonlight, leaving all my work behind.
Where am I going? To Caol Acainn. Out to the edge
Of the world I'll go, I'll see the Black Isles with snow
In their folds, eat an orange, get a dress with fine lace on it,
Ride in carriages, and don so fine a cloak and bonnet
I'd not dare to show them in the church. Our Bess says
A man named Martin has made a book about us.
I wish to have a book. A boy with eyes like summer dreams
Of me, I know. Beneath bright leaves we'd stroll, and scheme
To kiss. I must go. And will I? Tomorrow I am seventeen.

22

[Signature illegible, ca 1744]

We are grateful for these lines, sent us by Fergus MacDonald. A colleague of Mairi MacIntyre, he was on St Kilda in 1987 and 1991 and thinks he may have given this page to her, though the note 'found between the stones in a dry-wall...' was probably copied, as it is in her own hand. The book referred to is Martin Martin's *A Late Voyage to St Kilda*, 1697. Caol Acainn's modern spelling is Kyleakin; a caol (Gaelic) is a narrow strait between islands or, in this instance, between the Isle of Skye and the mainland. It seems to us that the author of these lines was, untypically, educated, since while she does not achieve a sonnet, she attempts rhyme, and formal verse of fourteen lines. Mr MacDonald also made available a copy of a page that appears to be ca 1875, but it is so damaged and fragmentary that one can read but one line: 'Young Duncan will be marrying—on 30 August, if we get the barley in.'—Eds.

Unattributed Fragment (2)

Sister Mary Cairnith lit the lamps,
it being four o'clock and the gale come,
but not my man, no, he's nae come.

I watch her from my bed, the pains
thrumming through me like the sea
in waves. The bairn is dead. How strange

to be so empty and so filled with salty water.
The breasts will swell. It will again be hard,
none [words missing] needing suck, my daughter's

[heart?] stops . . .

No records of a Sister Mary Cairnith could be located. —Eds.

My Sister Anna Clare Writes from Lewis, November 1833

If we had wanted abundance I suppose
we could have chosen another home.
This place is full of losses. When the boat

went down in the Minch it was a clear day
and the sea looked green and flat from here
though the currents have a mind of their own

as you know, and take who they will.
It was our Francis, and I can't say
I had foreknowledge. The sky was clear

and my heart light too, like the shallows
you see through to sand, and no stones.
The seals had gone, and the razorbills.

We had no thought, except the ones
you always do, the worry whispering
like the sea when it's still—you always hear it.

Like a child itself, the sea is. Once he's born
you never don't think of him, never don't know
what he's doing. Living here is like that.

And it's beautiful. Even when you forget—we did
this time—its treachery. If you could spare a wee bit
of comfort on the next boat we would be grateful.

It has not been possible for us to locate the speaker or her sister. —Eds.

Alma Rose Writes from St Kilda, 1884

On the carriage on my way, [blots? clots?] of dark on the hills
—not cloud, [illegible] contend and sweep whole ranges
at their whim—heather before it wakes, which being strange
to hills like these and far from home, I didn't recognize. Not a
    little ill,

[several words missing] dreamed a woman at a well, a bad sign
[illegible] but I so ill it didn't matter. I did not fear to die
that day. At sea I was much sicker yet. It took more than a day
to get here, if it's a day while light remains. Thank God for eyes:

I fancy that they do not want to rest, but everywhere seek detail
—and all the weathers colour rock: clear days the stone is grey or
    blue,
like seas stopped and [several words missing] but in the mist
most common here—it's almost black. The colour and the view

make your heart heavy, but [illegible] sun-shine falls direct
and all the colours come up brilliant red. When I arrived
I didn't know this yet, and when I spied that dark steep rock
rising from the churning grey-green ocean empty as a stac

I had to keep from weeping. Now I've got used to it on Hirta,
hard work's brought fourteen children to the school.
I stay with a family named Cullen and their three wee boys
and I am doing useful work.

We study hard beside the manse. The minister comes by
each day to lead our prayers in the morning and at noon,
[illegible] at four before we go. They speak their own tongue here,
Gaelic mixed with words I do not know but have Norwegian
    [stock ?]

In books—my hoard so few, all of them damp and salty now—
I've [learnt?] that Norse had been the tongue of people here.
They have a strange soft lisp I find quite calming, and a music
marks their speech, a different [lilt?] from sounds on Lewis,

or home at Uist. Many want to stop them [using?] the old tongue
and say that Gaelic is for heathen, and a bar to progress,
but I believe the lullabyes and hymns, the songs that people sing
[whilst?] they [thresh?] dye and weave and put their bairns to sleep

should not be tampered with and are a part of soul.
We come to help and not [several words missing]
what is change? And is it good it brings? Till Christmas,
when I see you—if seas be calm and weather clear, Alma Rose.

Parish records show a Cullen family, eight children (two girls) born to Mary
Margaret (variously Ainslie or Ainsley) Cullen and her husband Andrew (born
1857), of whom three survived. Information that the school once had fourteen
pupils, as well as the folk-belief that seeing a woman washing at a well prefigures
a death appear in *Island on the Edge of the World: The Story of St Kilda*, by
Charles Maclean. Readers should note that spelling (Mrs Cullen's name, Ainslie,
Ainsley) has still not been standardised in rural parts of the country. —Eds.

Mr MacAndrew Writes from St Kilda, 1892

I have put aside all thoughts of helping these people.
Their Accusations are untrue and I repudiate them!

Outrageous, Sir. Such rash complaints are Scurrilous,
without Foundation. The girl is young and plain. Sir,

She does not bathe. A little Child, she is one of my Flock
for whom I care, and with whose Care I am most Seriously

Charged in True Holy Obligation. She is not my equal
in works of the Mind, nor womanly in her Response

or Thought of her Religious resolution. Therefore
I shall leave here to Do Gods Work elsewhere. Please

arrange my passage at the soonest Opportunity
and find a Parish—with a Simple Manse in the Highlands

where I can be at Home. Or, if Your Grace please
I might heed a calling to the City, brown

though it is, full of vice and foreigners and crowds,
who do not speak our Gaelic—as all do here. I require

very little and am Grateful for Your Confidence. If Your Grace
would give my Most Affectionate Regards to Your Wife

and Daughters I would be Most Highly Pleased. Your Faithful
Servant, Reverend George Mac Andrew of Dunblane.

We believe this is one of the letters Mairi MacIntyre composed—perhaps with
the help of her American friend—in the voices of clergymen (see MacIntyre's
fourth letter to her husband, beginning 'Alec, old dear'). There had been in the
news during the weeks prior to MacIntyre's visit to St Kilda, a spate of articles
about the abuse of children by their pastors, both in the US and in Europe. —
Eds.

Mary Angela Rose Writes from St Kilda, 1903

You think because I am a midwife I will talk of babies lost
that came in winter squalls, their mothers without milk,
the blood, white thighs. No. Though I admit the thighs will

sometimes move me. And the bairns. A person is not made
of stone. They wail. I oil and swaddle them. I study
small pale faces and sometimes I can tell the ones will live

a week, a year, and aye, I grieve over wee hopes lost,
the man he would have been, the bonnie lass. Here am I
with three names, a richness that discomforts me

in this poor place. My mother died as I saw light: in prayer
my father gave me holy names and bright, and in my time
I have replied to all of them. I no longer fancy living here

though on the mainland I would always be a stranger.
Here the land is fine, all stones and hills, but steep: hard to climb,
      hard
on the feet, hard to farm. Like a picture of my loneliness.

It may be on the mainland there'd be others more like me.
I like to watch the sun rise from the sea but not go into it,
and never look west: it's too empty. In all these years, only one time

did I bring out an unnatural child. Several born dead or marked,
but only one affrighted me. Afterwards I had bad dreams.
I was sitting on the beach—I never would do—and a boat,

tossed ashore, splintered and threw pieces on me, spar
and ropes and boards and nets: I sat in ruins under stars
as cold as sin. Then things of metal fell out of the sky

—but how could they?—stone and metal cannot fly
like birds. Rock and metals fell. They crushed
the sheep and tore the grasses, leaving gashes on our island.

Once I married but my husband went away to Shetland.
I felt for many years that I disgusted him. Even clean
I smelled of blood and milk. My work reminded him

of troubled ways that men and women come together.
Once I saw him watching sheep. I saw his mouth
all twisted, though he didn't know it. When birds come south

I sometimes think of him. Once a stick, I have grown stout
and I wonder what it would have taken. Perhaps nowt
would join us—even wee ones of our own—if he had remained.

To the Editors from Mairi MacIntyre's Mother, Mary Rose MacIntyre, 17 January, 1995

Sirs [sic],

My childhood was filled with stories of the 'flu epidemic of 1918–1919. My mother, Mary Ross, was born in I think 1917, but her mother, Margaret Anne Smith, who had been born around the turn of the century, would have been almost a grown young woman when the 'flu began. She lived through it, and from the way my mother talked, I always fancied my grandmother was afraid to lose my mother and her brothers (they were babies) to the 'flu—in much the way we worried before the polio vaccine. One winter day—I remember ice ticking on the glass and snow was blowing hard, but did not stick—my mother said she thought her mother might've lost someone she loved. You mean a man? I said, stretching my mind to see Grandmother young, but my mother fell silent then, and I have no evidence at all—

[Signed]
Mary Rose MacIntyre

Hill Rose Cottage
Sea Road
Nairn

Mrs MacIntyre refers to the Spanish 'flu pandemic, now thought to have 'jumped' from swine to humans. —Eds.

Mr John Blair Writes from St Kilda, 1924

I fear that I must write the truth, however rough.
The people here are backward, though they've grown
accustomed to travellers coming to take photographs
and buy their woven cloth of quite fine quality,
and Sundays in my church they are devout enough.

I notice quiet dramas in the lives of every little clot
and gathering. One senses heaving, like the sea
beneath, of much not said, and troughs of feeling.
In winter months they do not bathe as we do,
and have other habits I would rather not refer to.

One wants to help, but they do not permit a stranger,
though needs be known, to them as well: bairns die,
the midwife has but roots for remedy, and Lister's name
has not been spoken here. The place has been passed by.
I tend my flock as best I can, but truly, spirit falters. History,

like progress, has quite shunned this little island.
To soothe my soul I study works of God's great hand:
down at the edges of the rock the sea's a miracle of clarity,
and birds above in bright extraordinary numbers fly.
I do not ask it easily: please see how soon you can replace me.

Monsignor Benveniste Writes from Lewis, 1937
[Fragments]

. . . as for sending a priest out to St Kilda, I would not
encourage it; it's a hard place for young men.
Our records show visits in 1896 and prior
as well as [word missing] this century. Stout hearts
may find it challenging, but not productive.
If you've a zealous man, he might do something there.
The island is spectacular, the ocean famously clear,
with [word missing], whirlpools, eddies round the stacs,
exceptional bird-life, and not a little weather.
A young man so inclined and with an interest
in the natural world might cast his line
for souls for Rome whilst learning about rural folk—
Gaelic speakers all—and bring a bit of comfort
to people starved, dispirited and quite alone
from one year to the next. . . . [Several lines missing]
. . . late in the day, since our brothers
in the Protestant clergy [word missing] Yours in Christ.

[Signature illegible, probably Anthony] Benveniste

Barbara Rose Writes from South Uist, 1943

It's been cold here and hard, with the war
going on and the sea not safe. Of course
it never was safe, but those were dangers
we could understand. I'm taking time out

from the weaving and the war to write you
a confession, Margaret, dearest cousin.
I thought everything that could happen
had happened. You remember the U-boat

shelled the wireless on Hirta in '18. Then
in '25 we left and came to South Uist,
a good place, but not home, and different.
Fifteen I was then, met my man and married him

in a fine ceremony in the church you missed
because of the storm that kept you
on the mainland. Perhaps I should come
to you there. Will you tell me what to do?

At times I wonder we haven't got confession
in our church—then I thank the Lord!
I can't talk to Mr MacArthur, it's too ugly.
I need to write it down and tell it just to you.

Francis has not left me but I wish he would.
Has found another. This is shame
and humiliation. As you know, it's all stones
here. Now that's all I see. I have a vision

that returns: everybody standing on the beach
whilst they bring his body in, but if that happened
I couldn't bear the children crying. I want things
as they were between us, warm and bright.

We had a quiet comfort. Soon the children
will find out. What will be? The sea
is blue and green today, and full of secrets.
I wish I had the courage to walk into it

but that's a sin. I can't leave this terrible life
or the bairns. These days I wish for feathers
to soar above the islands and the open sea
safe, aloft in all that wild blue, untethered.

Postcard to Steven from Skye, 1973

Am sending—soon as I can copy it—a letter found in a bench
in a church near Waternish—so old! Someone must've hidden it—

Finally got here!!! It's as Dick says, surpassing.
Camped in Portree, properly Port Righ, the king's
port, a little harbor called the capital. Great
craíc and folk music at the Tongadale Hotel
till midnight, when the light went, finally.
I'm learning Gaelic, which they call "gallic" here.
You have to see light pooling on the water, gold.
Molten sun, but cold, and steams. Love, Maggie

Craíc in Gaelic (pronounced crack) means fun and drinking, jokes, a convivial
time. We infer from the unremarkable image on the reverse, and from the double
inverted commas, that the writer was an American visiting the island; we do not
think she is someone known to Mairi MacIntyre, who would have been thirteen
in 1973. —Eds.

Maggie's Find on Skye

Good Brother in Christ, Greetings! Our Lord
in his Goodness Must drive out Despair
And my Soul Punish it. I am Out-Toun, a Field
Outlying. Perhaps if my People had Lived in This Place—
They are My People after All, in God, and by Nation.
It is only a few Years since Wee Joined our Fate to Englands
but These remain Strange. After bending Back and Neck
Yea All my Bodys Strength Chopping at the Ice in Souls
with Christs Help finally I Broke it all Away
and with my Bare hand Brushed the Surface.
Heere, I said, At last, fine sparkling Crystals!
My Heart eased. I leant to look. Before my Eyes
lay Granite. God in His Mercy Knows Why
He Suffers mee Heere. May Hee Bless and Keep You.

—A'^{d}r McGillivr^{a}y

This is probably authentic. Since Maggie is American, she would not know 'out-toun,' but we infer this from its faithful spelling and punctuation that she was a student or scholar. We also feel confident in asserting that since it has been copied in ballpoint in a modern hand on contemporary paper, it is probably Maggie's fair copy. In 1973 there were no photocopy machines on Skye. —Eds

Bill Writes Home from Harris, 1989

Mother's funeral is done. Home's unfamiliar now
though not much changed except for tourists
but one can't complain. It's not a little odd
to find three aging women where my sisters were.
The children all live on the mainland now
and I can't comment, having left as well. The boats
that Gil and Bob and Simon owned are sold;
they work for shipping companies and telephone.
All their sons—surprising me—are grown
much taller than their fathers. Gold-red gods they are,
working at Caledonian MacBrayne and stealing hearts.
Every night they're in the pubs. My own are spent
reading and sketching. An occasional pint.
Too much television and not enough music, but part
of each day I am down at the water, which remains.
Tomorrow I go down to see Aunt Mary at Mallaig,
then Uncle Fraser and Aunt Meg. No one else's left.
I miss you. This might well be my last trip home.

This seems quite definitively by Mairi MacIntyre. Though it is perhaps less artful
than her other work, we include it because our colleagues felt it captured the
loss islanders have experienced in this century, both those who leave and those
who stay behind. —Eds.

Mairi MacIntyre: To Iain Fraser
from Inverness, 1992

We reproduce this Application for the dig on St Kilda in its entirety as it sets out a bit of MacIntyre's family history as well as her motivation for, and commitment to, the study. As will become clear in the pages following, MacIntyre must somehow have discovered—or created?—her grandfather's indiscretion. If true, one can imagine its effect on the writer more than fifty years on. —Eds.

Dear Mr Fraser: Please consider this request
to join the study session on St Kilda. An architect,
I have built on Harris and have three times
—*The American says my letter is a poem
    and broke it into lines!*—
been to South Uist to study vernacular buildings

for my article which appeared last year
in *Scotland Only / Yesterday* (enclosed).
My father's mother, Barbara Rose,
was born on St Kilda and left in 1925.

She is buried in South Uist. I have lately found
her copy-book—it is stuffed with folios
and sketches, indecipherable notes. Barbara Rose
survived, the only one of seven children,

so my father thinks. None were sons.
Pages tell of shawls from Glasgow, lengths
of linen from Belfast, a silver pin
from Oban. As I read, her days rise

to the present to disturb what lies beneath, like tides.
'We scrubbed the poison out' she writes
of a blue bottle—perhaps for medicine?—
'stood it in the window that opens the west wall.'

There are drawings of the village, detailed
renderings of cleitan with significant attention
to arrangements of the stones. Sometimes I think
my profession came to me, I didn't choose it.

Who knows what we choose. Her name
does not appear anywhere on the pages
but initials intertwined with flowers, B and R,
in fading soft-blue ink appear occasionally.

I am fortunate to have these pages, stained
and fragile as they are. The copy-book
is full of hymns and prayers, sketched pods
and leaves. The front is labelled 'Barbara Rose',

Her Book, and was a kind of journal. She married
Francis MacIntyre, who came, I think, from Jura.
I want to find her parents' names.
Working on St Kilda I am certain I'd reclaim

a history that's part of me, that I must find.
I want to make a gift of family story
to my mother, now my father's gone.
I can meet with you at any time.

Most sincerely, Mairi MacIntyre

We have reproduced Mairi MacIntyre's own placement of the note (which interrupts stanza 1) on the page.

Cleitan (stanza 6) are small drystone buildings designed to let the wind blow through in which people kept vegetables and grain, peat and hay.

We are grateful to Mr Iain Fraser for his willingness to permit publication of this private communication. —Eds.

Mairi MacIntyre: To Her Mother
from St Kilda, 1994

Dearest Mum. I'm on the site at Gleann Mór
on Hirta. It's astonishing and empty here.
I can't say I feel souls—even in a wave
or on the air—of the great-grandparents.
I wish they'd lived to know their girl is here.

Stony hills plunge hard to sea, the rock
straight walls in places; cliffs' faces pocked
and carved repeat the falls beneath the sea
which they are still a part of. Fowlers,
the St Kilda men would climb them!

On our way I asked to see Stac an Armin
but with ocean rough, waves high
—dark-green like bottle-glass—and fog
blowing in like curtains off the sea
we had to make landfall whilst it was still possible.

I've a flickering Coleman but at ten o'clock
it's not much needed. The sky here is immense
but not so wild—without the land to argue with
it's not so turbulent as it will be at home.
Alec didn't want to let me go but his people

have always lived on the mainland
so he can't understand, and perhaps
I should not expect it? We've agreed
I'll come out every summer for a month
as long as the digs last. This is a right

proper link to my work on Scottish buildings.
I have climbed the earth berm, been to
Tigh an Triar, sat on rock and stared out
at the sea, but not yet been to Lover's Stone.
The views are dizzying to Ruaival and Dùn.

I do love digging here among the stones,
as if I'll soon find evidence of Barbara Rose
or Francis, and then I'll know what calls me.
I like my colleagues, who seem fun, and quick
— though to expect some briars seems realistic—

Hugs, darling-Mum. Mairi

Oh, I forgot to say: beneath the water-line the stac,
196 metres—tallest in Britain—is a sharp knife-edge,
one can land only if the wind's in the north-west.

P.S. Again—Consult the map I made you, Mum!

The berm is an earthen dyke which forms a continuous wall round the head of Gleann Mór (The Great Glen). Tigh an Triar, House of the Trinity, is an unusually large cleitan leading to Gleann Mór. For a description of this part of Hirta, see David Quine, *St Kilda*, whom we cite here.

We have interleaved among the letters several pages of Mairi MacIntyre's journals, dreams and fragments. Maps and drawings accompany many of these personal pages. It is clear that MacIntyre, perhaps because of her training in architecture, took great pleasure in her drawings, for they range from the immensely detailed and graceful, putting one in mind of Turner's sketches, to the quick line-drawing which shows her easy humour. Insufficient funds preclude our reproducing these, which may be seen by visiting the appropriate libraries.
—Eds.

From Mairi MacIntyre's Journals (1)
[No date]

Sometimes a band of white or gold or rose
on the horizon; otherwordly green, turquoise,
or a hard sheen—like jasper—on the sea
seems the Aurora come to earth to wrap me
in a gleam like the interiors of shells:
moonstone, feldspar, tuff, white jade. They melt,
then pour like streams out of the rock, pure light.

I would walk in to the flare of that embrace,
cool echo of the blare and clamour of the Sun:
the most extraordinary thing we've seen
and we can't look at it straight on—God's face.

Mairi MacIntyre: To Margaret Adams
from St. Kilda, 1994 (1)

Margaret-my-love, what would I do
without you to talk to? Alec
was furious when I left but I must
come, must do this work, hard
as it is on a land mean enough
to break your heart and beautiful.
How could they fancy they could wrest
food and a living from this place?
Of course they couldn't; left.

[In ink of another colour MacIntyre
has interrupted herself to add
a mid-letter afterthought. —Eds.]

I find m'self obsessed with isolation—drawn to & horrified—
wish you could see the way the island drops or tumbles
spills
hurtles
straight down to the sea—

We are eight here now (the numbers fluctuate),
an American who's nice enough, quiet—for them—
and smart. I find myself drawn to a photographer,
male, alas, but will not act upon 't. Alec
will be travelling so I can't fathom why
he provoked such trouble. Today we found
two small baptismal artefacts. Most of the children died
of tetanus at eight days. I can't imagine how they stayed. Mairi

Mairi MacIntyre: To Her Husband
from St Kilda, 1994 (1)

My love. You'd hate it here: flies and the wind
blowing all the time. I'm happy out in the middle
of the Atlantic, on the middle of my island.

'My' indeed! I write late at night in fine soft light
before I fold myself into my tent. I think this work
will still that restive thing in me that so disquiets

you. Gleann Mór was a shieling. Even now
descendants of the early sheep: feral
creatures populate the land like stones.

We found a quaich today—great celebrating!
During a brief hard rain I considered sheltering
in a cleitan but resisted the temptation.

Lead me not. There are remains of many kinds
of buildings we are looking at; the burial ground
is in a little walled space like a broch.

I miss you. I wish you'd been here to meet
the American archaeologist. She tells me people stare
when they hear her accent—which is quite flat,

none of it's rounded properly. We don't stare,
she said. How do you look at people, then?
Sidewise, she said. These are direct Americans!

Told me she understood perhaps eight percent
of what's said here though it's English, was relieved
when I said, No, it's Scots, and told her how the language

recollects its old Norwegian music. Tomorrow
we meet in the Village where we plan to analyse
the shape of settlement. Sometimes my eyes

tear and I'm glad of the wind: we are near the edge
where a great trench falls almost two hundred metres
to sea-floor. Imagine little groups of people sheltering

briefly here. I can see them, braced against the wind
on this wee dot made of rock—though small,
it can change the weather round the stacs.

As you asked, I'm taking photographs. Love, Mairi

Quaich: a small chalice used for baptism, esp. when the clergyman came to the
house to administer the sacrament there. A broch is a fortification (thought to be
first-century) found most notably on Orkney. —Eds.

From Mairi MacIntyre's Journals (2)
[8 August]

When ice breaks you gaze into blue water.
Forced to watch as it grows wider.

Long pause while I think

Not only times with Alec.
This is how I leave my Mum
—or she leaves me.
It's how age comes.

Mairi MacIntyre: To Her Husband
from St Kilda, 1994 (2)

My love, greetings from my island. Mine indeed.
The American's interesting, loves to practise
rolling r' s, says all those photos of the women
brought her to the island, 'silent Presby-teeerrr-ians'

she smiles, concerned about offending. Sitting
in a row against their rocks, the women
look as if they never speak—but there are children—
or they are in the background with their knitting.

She said, 'The women were silent but their hands
were not, and rocking cradles was the least of it.'
She wants to imagine their lives and write
them—quite a reach I'd say, but give it a go.

An academic and a writer. You might like her.
The work is teaching me another kind of being: slow,
it frustrates one at first, and one must wait
on others, but I'm learning patience, how

to tarry, perhaps I shall think differently.
In a sense the dig is science even prior
to the time we classify and analyse.
There was a galey day but most are clear.

The light on hills and water takes the breath
and heart. I don't know why I've never thought:
in old days explorers had among them artists
to record 'exotic' places (an ugly word

I don't much care for anymore), but in our time
photographers chronicle, computers archive
—a loss of texture, both of paper and of cloth,
to the hand as well as eye—but of course

one can't go back. Sixteen days and I'll be home
though if tides and wind do not permit
it might be longer. One gives oneself over to what is.
You might not even get this letter. Love

They Come Ashore (1)
[August 1994]

in my dream, in the dark, the people
taken off the stac. Candles flare
above the sea and dance in air
like the spirits who will sing them home,
the hearty and the frail, their faces ovals
in the dark, another dark, unsmiling.

Gratitude requires too much effort.
Elbows jutting, boys watch; the men don't speak.
Clouds gather heavy silver-grey. Women heap
the food on platters it takes two to carry,
set them out on tables balanced on flat stones
in the dark that answers their dark clothes—

From Mairi MacIntyre's Journals. A small group of these were titled by MacIntyre herself and dated with month and year; we have reproduced them as we found them. It will be seen that the dream refers to events of 1727. See 'Mary Clare Writes from Uist, 1730.' —Eds.

They Come Ashore (2)

This appears to hve me 'by the throat'
—as the American says.

My dream had got the details wrong:
the women had been sick, were grieving,
were too few for feasts, had not the strength

to carry food in heaps. In the event
they hadn't much. The dream
was full of mediaeval overtones, capes, green

hoods soft as velvet, tapers flaring,
shadows like the ones I've seen
in countless films which train

—or ruin—the eye. Or: the mood
more properly defines the dig,
time and settlement: people've lived

on St K since the Iron Age,
which reminds: Our American
tasted Ir'n Brew and hated it.

How does it taste to you?
Nods premature apology,
says *Rusty nails* and laughs,

Steeped for weeks in Royal Crown
Cola, which you could only get in the South
I come from, but perhaps not anymore

—which would not be a major loss.
I'd send you some, but customs men
might think it's diesel fuel or gasoline,

which brought us to the tracks of whales
—she called them *footprints*—
oily stains on the surface of the sea—

    Been thinking what would have happened if they
    weren't brought in, if there had been a late winter
    and the boat not come in time. . . Woke before
    dawn in floods of tears
    —it will be hard to go home—

Mairi MacIntyre: To Margaret Adams from St Kilda, 1994 (2)

Margaret-love. You must burn this
—or chew it! Remember those spy
tales? People wrote in milk or urine,
warmed it over heat—a light bulb,
or a candle—watched the words appear.

Not urine. Blood, likely: mine.
Torches turn all the tents
to *luminaria*—or visitors
from Venus shining in the dark.
The photographer, Arne,

squatted in the doorway to my tent,
his back to my small fire beyond.
Is he here to warm his bum? I thought.
A Swede, he's lived in Scotland
30 years—he's 42. So: squats.

Makes not-brilliant small-talk. Sparks,
a few quite bright but scarce, fly.
Then he pauses, says, *Well, Lass?* and I,
throat stopped, who meant to say
quite soft, *Come in* could not.

From Mairi MacIntyre's Journals (3)
[No date]

—pull exerted by photography—not the photographer!
    [p]hotographs are art?

camera shows what's already there.

                A man (or of course woman) chooses or arranges.

Is Art The Moment Captured Or The Moment Made?

A man falls from a building. Someone with a camera follows the
    trajectory
and sells the film to television. A child covered with napalm
    burning runs
down a road. This makes a difference to the people running
the war. Does it make it art? A definition
I read somewhere: Rescue From Oblivion. *Can't forget*

all sorts of things of no significance, the grey-green leaf-
imprinted stone from Birsay Graeme gave me, a dress
when I was four: scatterings of little roses
on a woven striped white ground. Junk Dreams, *Graeme said*
lifting a pint. Photos make junk memories—
ones we think we had but had not, recollections without weight
    or history—

                — if Arne knew I Thought *these things—!*

Mairi MacIntyre: To Her Husband
from St Kilda, 1994 (3)

Alec—I hadn't thought to tell you this.
The American said 'Know what I miss?'

(They leave off words, and shorten
those they do use.) 'It's never silent here.

And those damn birds!' A gesture, white hand
imitating flight, 'And the ocean grinding stone

away, making tonnes of sand.'
It does that: grind. Sometimes the thunder

of the waves stuns. Sound bangs and claps
like an articulated lorry's sudden stop,

shuddering and rattling
in a great sea-voice. Nature ought

be still? said I, surprised, which sent her
into a long riff (she plays the guitar,

and the photographer has brought a banjo
though both complain they don't stay tuned

in all the damp) about '*commuuuuning*',
being '*at one with*', delivered broad,

theatrically and warm. Perhaps she'll come
to us next year. I shall invite her! Love

From Mairi MacIntyre's Journals (4)
[No date]

The train-ride out to Skye [illegible] and blots
of dark [two lines illegible] and then recalled
my awful dream: in negative, sled dogs
all white on a dark ground—I know it's snow
despite the colour. Rottweilers, Ridgebacks
bred to bring down lions—Alsatians in their traces
lunge and pull and howl. And then
the leather harness melts, as dreams allow,
they leap in graceful arcs and float, then fall
and I am meat for hungry mouths, *horror!*
puppies [illegible] fluffy dears have changed:
big cats pour down on me like rain.

The American says
You're afraid, and *Why is that a problem?*
Well, it is. I wanted to come here—

She laughs, says: *Things*
you can't say after Freud:
I want my father. I didn't mean. . .
I know.

Said we'd sing it,
put it all to pipes, had we the pipes—!

She tells us not a lot
about herself but I fancy her
in tattered dresses in the 60's,
long skirts, a glass of red wine

in a slender hand, and her thick curls.
Her hair is light and thinning

and her face shows age.
I think—I!—that I will live forever!

What madness keeps us from imagining our age?

The train does not go to Skye. From Inverness, one must take a bus, or drive. Since MacIntyre lived in Inverness we assume this to be a bit of the sort of thoughtless rapid compression often found in journals and dreams. —Eds.

From Mairi MacIntyre's Journals (5)
[No date]

I suppose the American is right: dreamed
I was on St Kilda in a gale without my anorak
or boots—no gear for rain, nor pack
nor food, in a worn wee jersey and a little skirt.
No torch. Old fears return
in local guise, specific and expert.

Mairi's Drafts

What fun! A group I'll call 'Foundations'

Oslo, 923

Crusty snow shines like a bowl
hardened by the fire,
hurts the eyes but pleases soul.

In the spring the longboats
carry us to meeting, but now we ski
through night to the gathering

that marks the darkest time. All night
we'll sing and pray—for light
to return and berries, for water

to run, bright fish to leap
where we can take them. The birds
will come if our gods please,

and bees fill the air with humming.
My Erik-Aage was told a holy thing:
a new Lord brings the summer

and we must make the god good welcome
in all the places we have seen the sacred
with wine and singing, meat and bread

to feed him. I do not like the rise
of a distress in me, uneasy sleep, dread
pictures in the night and cries,

Aage: the younger. —Eds.

as if the wolves in packs were on their way.
With proper care the god will bless, they say,
and if we make right prayers and sacrifice

then he will make the winter go
like ice becoming flowers of snow
then water, sweet and clear and flowing.

Oslo, 1085

Olaf and Erik go south when the sun
climbs and I am left behind to pray
for them. Now the men say
we must love the Christ or die,
or if not die, be punished. They show
a man bent double underneath
the new lord's feet. I do not know
how this can happen, though
his new church stands foursquare
and sturdy and the wood smells sweet.

Fires soon enough will darken
walls and carvings. My lord Olaf
made the faces on the west
and southern walls. The north
where evil comes from none would touch.
I stitch fine blossoms on a cloth
for the tall and reaching altar
we have painted red and blue and gold
but in my heart's own winter core
I know I love the old gods more.

Oslo, 1407

When Erik sails for the New World
he means to take his sister. My heart
will split like wood beneath the axe.

Men returning sing breaches in the earth
that steam and send up water all in colours,
springs that froth and boil and smoke,

and not a tree. They go out in the boats
and the gods take them: all do not come home.
Here we are safe beneath the hills

where our fortress guards the sea.
Some nights when I drive the cattle in
I hear a stirring in the wind

under the thud of their hooves
and the mooing. Foolishness! There are loaves
to be kneaded and baked, fish

to be salted. Sometimes at night I look
and in the winter sky and dancing lights
my man shines in the blue and pink like ice

with low sun on it. The sounds return
beneath the clamour of the wind, cries
beyond volition for my Erik's father—

and my girl's—who gave me six children
asleep beneath the sea and in the earth,
who spoke his heart, thus honoured me,

and fed me honeyed wine to ease each birth.
If he were here to hear me in the byre
his heart would weep, his eyes go dark

with that sweet fire and he would kiss
my neck and deeply warm me. Peace.
I have forty-two winters and work I must do.

From the two who remain to me
some comfort is necessary,
but Erik is young and headstrong,

and as she sews the girl chants
little story-songs of places far from home.
Perhaps she'll marry and bear sons

in the new land, good men like her father,
at ease in lands I shall not know.
I will prepare the bone and ornament,

bowls and cutting tools, dried meat,
furs she'll take across the sea.
O Christ! I send her far from me.

Iceland, 1410

[Illegible: Mine?] will be the last wedding
in this place we have tried to make a home.
Stones fell from the roof in the last storm
leaving spaces like odd windows—
through them one can see the sky!
Here even clouds are different and the ocean
not so friendly as at home. Nights I long
for my Baltic sky shining with silver. Church is cold
but brighter than the wooden ones at home,
their staves all dark and tarry from the fires.
Bjørn does not want to go back. This night
I will share his bed. When I let him
put his hand into my furs I burned wonderfully.

Mairi MacIntyre: To Mr William Boyd
from St Kilda, 1994
[Excerpts]

    ... getting away was a bit dodgy
(I suppose it always will be)
—then I was on the *Sutherland*
in quite extraordinary seas—and here!
. . . .
[she mentions Festival, and adds]
I miss a lot avoiding Edinburgh in August
but see what I've arranged this year
. . . .

This place haunts and hurts
. . . .
I would be nowhere else.

In the Village the remains of rows
of undressed stone declare how little buildings matter,
as you tried to teach us—at the same time
that they matter greatly. . . . What's left,
windows, lintels: open doorways into mist and sky,
chimneys guardians whose charges all have left . . .

We are grateful to Mr William Boyd, Mackintosh Professor of Architecture, University of Aberdeen, who has kindly permitted excerpts we have included here.
—Eds.

From Mairi MacIntyre's Journals (6)
[Date illegible]

A fierce storm nearly carried my tent downhill
with me inside! Quite clear, a woman's voice:
Heaven broke and raved and cried. Skies
tore and crashed and split: such tumult
seemed to say we're not meant to dig here.
I felt the breath of warning faeries, and those men
who live beneath the earth in Norse tales, foolish
girlhood stuff inappropriate for a grown
and educated woman as the century nears its end.

Someone (aye!) has overturned a sea and yet another
sea. As if the world had spilled and every solid's water,
walls of ocean rage and fall—they do not pour—
thick fury loosed. The notion they carve gullies
down to sea and in the night the very land I (barely) rest on
changes quite amazes me. Tomorrow gashes
will have cut the land, muddy raw and terrible:
in crevices I'll see the burning dark interior: skins
that hold the world had peeled away and floated free.

Mairi MacIntyre: To Her Husband
from St Kilda, (4) 1994

Alec, old dear. I miss you. The weather's changed
dramatically, as it will do when autumn sweeps
down from the north, which is quite present here.
Skies are shuttered, summer's past. Clouds scowl,
chastise and forbid. My friendly American has gone,
but hopes to come again next year: the bonnie *Sutherland*
took her and several others home.

[Lines following appear to have been written at a different
time and with a different pen, though in MacIntyre's
unmistakeable hand. —Eds.]

                    Find myself
imagining lives of those who first came here,
a kind of counter or addition to the work she's done.

And have added—you shall see!—a group of clergymen . . . !

You Go Back

You go back to where people know
what has happened to you.

—must tell this to M[argaret]. . .

[drawing of tents and hills; the view
is from the Village Well]

We slept in daylight, could do
no work, cloud low
today and wicked cold.

I dreamed hot baths and towels
thick enough and deep.

[sketch of bath-tub; cartoon,
overleaf, of woman wrapped
in a very large spotted towel]

In childhood [words missing]
of sleeping on a cloud but the reality
is fearful—fraught, and not the fluff [or stuff]
of girlhood reverie. I was driven to see
how far away all that is now,
how incomprehensible the space
we occupy. And as for us, who knows
what we are. Yesterday I watched
a goat (terrible smell!) and wondered
what it sees through those barred eyes.

[Water-stains and smears of blue ink:
it appears that two lines are missing]

I was thinking this when the American
quoted a book she'd brought along:
Brazilian woman considering
an egg: 'if I were to understand
the egg, it could only be in error.'
What could this *mean?* she said.
We laughed
    [Illegible; words missing]
             voices
like sounds of faeries
playing in a glen, beyond
a stand of trees, at water's edge,
and we were wrapped in mystery,
as if our voices danced.

          —I heard us from quite far away,
          two women in the mist, disembodied
          —girlish voices.

This journal entry from the sketch-book is ornamented and enlivened by draw-
ings in coloured pencils, indicated. The book referred to is Clarice Lispector's
Selected Cronicas, published in the UK in 1991 by Carcanet Press as *Discov-
ering the World*. Readers of the New Directions edition (New York) will find the
quoted material on page 78. —Eds.

Eventually They Come Ashore

the living and the dead
whether you wait for them or not.
There are so many more
of the dead, and the living
drown on stony ground in grief
and anger, and the sea
does not care. We care
for it so deeply, need it
so we cannot comprehend
its treachery. We think
it must be part of Mind
and would not so mistreat us

but it closes its blue eyes,
a shunning, so defeats us.

BOOK II

I LIVE PAST YOU

August Morning

The sun beats the water to hammered aluminum
and two lifeguards rush down to the sea. I stop
to watch the rescue; shapes of recollection surface

after almost fifty years: my mother bent over a swimmer
she has hauled from the depths, working till he breathes.
Now a group of lifeguards, kids at summer work, collects

beneath the tall white chair, hands up to shield their eyes
from glare. Did he wave, or was he simply out too far,
too long, alone? One swimmer's reached the troubled one:

a wave goes up, but not the jubilation I expect, and then
the work begins. With nylon cord I can't discern from where I stand
the youngsters who remain on shore begin to reel him in. Hand

over hand they circle up and down the sand like dancers
in Virginia Reels, or relay racers handing on a slim baton.
At last the one far out is near, can stand, walk in,

and then I understand: a decoy rescue. It always takes too long
to see. Fallen and drawn down beneath a wall of foam,
taking in the elemental taste and pulse, without reason

you will fight to live. You're supposed to
concentrate on the rescue. In bright sun, shade
of the only woman's face I have ever longed to press my mouth to,

bent to save a stranger. The youngsters bleach and burnish
in the sun: forms who've fled the pipes and song
of ancient urns come to us dancing, hand the invisible line along.

Migrations

In fast hearts of birds, heads of whales, breasts
of reindeer, as rubies gather light and bind it, embers
like roses of hot coal show the way home
along threads of clear silk, mesh we have imagined
and stretched over the incomprehensible curves
of the world. Skies fill with cries: returning
storks, flamingos, terns. And people,
as their planes cross the equator, pulled
full awake as to true north, point at which all forces
gather and disperse. As mass deforms
the space around it, you divert streams
in the surrounding air and I am pulled beyond volition home.
Compelled or drawn to one man's ordinary and familiar arms
to open unconstrained like rosy paper flowers aflame.

Flight Paths

I wait in yet another airport for a man. BOS,
Denver, LAX. Once again I am aloft

and grounded. Flight-besotted men sky-dive,
pilot little open breezies, sail their gliders

through the turbulence of skies, ride
currents exigent as appetite astride

the wild rush of streams in air, hands
steady on the steering-gear, breath barely

in control. Flight as metaphor and risk,
all that maleness rising out of rifts

defining personality the way the Great Rift
Valley opens Africa, its dark erratic slit

a feature visible from space. Space,
which is time, creases, folds, slips:

you sail into my life again, a streak of light,
and here it is, showy as anthurium; as if

it were apart from me I watch as it articulates,
discloses, heedless of decades or will as if

we are wholly matter strung on little frames
of bone, vivid and adrift in burning air.

Men Kneel

Like the unconscious and like art, beyond volition
and only partly human, what goes on
between men and women happens in the dark, feral,
without will. In gratitude or grief, at prayer,
before a bookcase seeking manuscripts or maps,
a man on his knees is entirely memorable.

Between my legs. Then humility opens in me
like a meadow, vast and blowy. Silky streaks
of limb, raw rutty bottoms: textures move us
to articulated knowing, acts pure, material,
blood fast and bright, arterial, that wild
indifferent sweetness when arousal takes us.

The Natural Element

You have no choice. This is as natural as breathing.
You let down into it or are drawn. Like heartbeat
it does not care what you think. Generated
in the salty marrow of your bones, radiant
with chemistry and synapse, old as seas, desire
wells up out of mystery and all proportion,
impersonal as history but sweeter, and close
as your own smells. It surges, swells
to take the shape of its container and spilling,
offers no apologies. It is not here for you
but uses you as it moves through, like music,
as insubstantial, as absolutely real.

True North

Years go. I drive the miles to where you wait for me,
marvelously male and bulky, unselfconscious.
Winds scour the gilded cumulus and rock the frame
of my car. What am I thinking? Mind's like sky.

Perhaps there've been a dozen days like this:
the world's griefs hover at a little distance
while we do common human things, one man,
one woman, all our mortal roaring stilled.

In every tale it's we who've made the world. World:
a cove of time, small haven open to the rain.
For a little while we're at the center
of a sphere of light, and Nemesis, the watching star

who circles like a lion waiting for the prey to fall
is for the moment far enough away and sleeping.

Weekend at the Beach

Also in the room but out of view, the man
I have not seen for nearly forty years and never will again.

At seventeen I could not have dreamed of this
—as in those days I was unable to imagine age. He comes

into the room, I rise to speak, and next
his mouth on mine, hands on my breasts.

Heedless of age and time we tumble to the bed
and I am laughing *Glasses!* as I push them to the edge.

Glasses once were raw discomfort. Where is shame
and why did I not celebrate its leaving? Time

gathers, curls and falls, and I am in the moment
—years and lives before—when, wearing a white dress

I never wanted, my new husband pressed
my breasts and shattered all the strangeness.

Beneath a sky like a van Ruisdael, clouds drift
as we do. I let down into it, as in more fluid days I slipped

into the Gulf off Florida, lifted in the vault
of blue, at home in buoyant seawash, phosphor, salt.

Mostly Sky

We eat lunch next to massive windows
out of which the sky and the Gulf float
equally blue and tangible. I say
I won't say anything personal.

You have always spoken code: numbers,
odds, and risk. *I've twenty percent of my heart.*
Weeping would be inappropriate here
and anyway, we have wept

as we have lived, separately. Florida
at Christmas. I am home. There
are wreaths, pinecones frosted gold,
sheer metallic ribbon twisted into bows.

You say *Don't you look out the window
at me.* I look. Like southern mornings
humid, cool, and dense, a faint mist
hangs between us, gauze in a breeze.

I watch it move above the tablecloth
and silver, fugue of recollected rapture.
Transformed, the need and crush
have worn now, pitted, like a mirror

into which we can see all the past
receding. Your hands on the tablecloth
are brown as earth
in orange groves. It was honey

but not sweet. It was air,
blue and white. It was cool and gleamed.
A marble tabletop, a threshold's edge,
a fiddle string, taut enough and waiting.

(On Not) Meeting David at the Beach

Silky-white, the sand I brush from my ankles sprays
like glitter on a clump of reddish grasses, airy,
bright. Before I speak the question you reply: *I expect
it's all been planted.* What are you doing here?

You appear like this. At the Glasgow School of Art
beneath the twisted tree that struggles in the well of stairs
facing the *Ancestors of Christ*, I thought you'd stopped
to talk with Mackintosh. You don't stay

where you belong, New York, my heart, but pop
into my life like something whimsical, part
time and bring time back togther like gauzy
theatre-curtains, as you did in life. Very near

to where I meet you here—if you try—
you can see me in the Gulf, fair child, distinct,
tossing a ball to her dog who circles her
in easy loops and arcs, the herding instinct

of some forebear married to a love for water. The sky
today's a darker echo of this empty stretch of beach
and placid as the sweetness after sex but colder.
I don't know why I didn't come to you in Barcelona

to sleep with you above the long brown sandy reach
that meets the fabled sea. I planned it all: the flight, white
dresses, espadrilles. I dreamed we'd make a girl-child there. Why
do we miss them, the dead? They go with us everywhere.

—*Midnight Pass, January*

Water's Edge

At the edge of the universe it's earlier than here
at the center of our lives, and in the infinite

interval between events our small lives go.
At Lake Michigan the size of inland seas surprises.

Raised on the Gulf coast, I'm not expecting tides,
geometries of gulls' prints, or this horizon

as it fades in sheens of haze. Days in late August
have a peculiar edge, as if, in the middle of the country,

you neared the limits of the world. At the edge of it
isolate light cries of foreign birds and tang of coming cold.

Time spins off the planet like red silk from a spool,
snaps and snarls. Memories unfurl. I walk through cool

exhalations like little breaths at water's edge
and across the event horizon to the place where all times fuse.

I am in bed with a man I have loved, or rapt
while he plays *Appassionata* for me. In the doorway

to the dining room I call out "Catch!" and toss a tangerine.
Every parting bends beneath the weight of permanent farewells.

All along the sandy verge I search a shape
that replicates a woman's curved form bent around the water.

Satellite Photo

—View from the south, over the Straits of Florida

Gleaming in its sheath of bluegreen air
and water, Florida's familiar body emerges
from black space and at the southeast edge

returns to it where the continental shelf
drops hard to darkness. The picture
doesn't show flat sandy country,

the wild variety of palm and fruiting trees,
the sprawling banyan at the Ringling Home
like circus elephants in stilled parade

around no tent. You can't see me walking
with an image of my mother, north
along a curve of Gulf, the water blue

as the insides of shells, as her eyes.
You can't see me spying—as when a fan
of palm fronds separates to let the wind

come through, or in a drift of vision
just beyond a clump of pines—Florida
in the forties and fifties, dusty, somnolent,

and dull, unselfconscious in its finery.
You can't see me leaving a man
I first loved thirty years ago and likely

will not see again. From 200 miles up,
what's visible: countless sweet blues,
the sandy littoral, swirls and brightness

in the shallows. Through cloud—fizz
like painted glitter on a painted sea—
erratic rounds of lakes, hammered silver

spangles planned, as for a necklace, in a row.
Then, the Maker suddenly distracted, dropped
at random all the way to Okeechobee,

just north of where the country hollows
like a bowl to hold the grassy inland sea. Home
hangs off the vast expanse of mainland

like a dollop of sweet cream or a drop
of seawater, heavy at the bottom, trailing
islands, a few drops blown to westward.

The Stunning

—Jeannie

As if a lost demented bee had stung
or evil fairy tossed a spell—soft cloth

that covers, stops—death stunned
an old friend into silence in a chopper

on her way for help. I call her name.
As if it were a choice she's made

and keeps on making she refuses
to reply. Like a dancer on a music-box

she whirls inside my mind as if it were a space
and fills it, her remembered voice like suede. Photos

show her holding my first living child. Now
except what I remember, nothing

of our years of easy interrupted talk remains,
kitchens seas of dirty dishes and soft foods—

bowls of cereal afloat in sour yellow milk
(semen dripping between our legs), skinned

peaches on the countertops, corn still sheathed
in green and underfoot all sticky, plums in pieces; heat

and toys; laundry stacked on floors and chairs.
Once I threw away a liquor base

for a dessert—pink liquid I had thought
was a detergent at the bottom of a heavy copper pot.

Beneath the hectic pleasures of those days
of fecund disarray, children's unremitting needs

and our talk sweet, when laughter screened
the hard things we were learning, could not say.

Starshine

Even on the deepest ocean you will be the light.
—Irish folk song: Dolores Keane

Once from a ship on the Baltic I saw
the permanent dark in its guise
as a night. At sea faint starshine
or a streak of phosphor in the rise
and fall of temporary mountains
gleams briefly if at all. Or it gleams
and you aren't there to see it
or it wasn't the right moment
when you looked. Sometimes I think
a man I loved is in the starry night, as if
when the car hit, his spirit, set adrift, lifted
and spun into light, as if he had become
a spray of shining like a fountain
and freed of flesh, his memory of me
—weeping, laughing, distant or aroused—
dissolved like snow-squall, brief fall
of light on seas of unspeakable dark.

Silk Dress

In my heavy new silk dress, dark blue,
I have come to know it fully: you are dead
beneath palm trees. Never the crush
of your arms, never your thigh thrust

between mine. Your voice never.
In my empty house I call your name out
—foolish girl—and like the girl I was
when you were here, shout. Echoes rush

into space like radio waves, straight off
into the dark where you are
where I will go, though not because you're there,

good dear, and I want you. I want you here
between me and the dark, quick
flesh, that fluttering small light, its guttering wick.

Lament in Three Cities

1. Edinburgh and Inverness

I picked poppies red as heartbeat
knowing they would stop within the hour.

I live past you. In the loch fish glitter
like rare metals and are gone.

2. Here

As I am always aware of New York to the east
where the sun comes from, ceaseless grit and clamor
all that ardent and unreckoned life
so you remain present at the periphery, rational as light.

Atlantic Beach

Dawn has come and gone but it is so early
that when I turn to see where I've come from
and where I will be going, it's still dark. I stroll
the narrow span between two great unknowns
toward where the sun unrolls
angled brilliants from her bolt of gold
and stop to watch gulls flitter above spitting foam
and sea, the thunder of its many tones
the music of the sphere we occupy. They hover
over swells like time stopped, or the heart,
then dive. Like boys who stand apart
from damages they do, they skim
the moving fields of blue as if killing were an art
and purpose and its deadly aim a part of joy.

Clay Figures

Now we know the people who made us
were merely children, afraid
we would find out how little
they were sure of, and like children
grown bored with their toys,
they have gone. We are the charms
they turned from and forgot;
if there were words to keep them
they've been lost. The wind picks up.
Hills and trees that slowed it are removed.
This is what we've always known:
they'd go out after dinner and not come home,
leaving us alone like small clay dolls
on the vast plain of the world. Now the draft
before the wide dismissive sweep
that one day will wipe us all away
the way a child's hand clears off a tabletop.

Kiln

Cave of earth and stone and hay. Den swept by fire
and storms. Hive domed like holy spaces in the west
of Ireland. Round: igloo, ger. Huts stepped
on steep terrain, a marching series of arcades
of mud and brick designed so rising currents drive
the heat uphill. Container for a local sun. Altar. Pyre.

Heat sheets the ware, pulls glaze from grains
of nickel, copper, lead, rare earths, weds the profane
to chance, and renders ordinary substances arcane,
brittle, brilliant; glass. Everything burns away.

The man you love is made of sandy clay, frit and stone,
bits of salt and ash. Open the door. What remains?
All you've ever known about him fades
before the dazzle of his presence in its house of bone.

Ceremonies of Bread and Wine

> *What shall I do...*
> *with all this immensity*
> *in a measured world?*
> —Tsvetayeva

1.

These dark smears are called flashmarks
and are thought to enhance the vessel.
This is the last whole object
out of the fire. See, it's flat
as a plate, made especially for you
from the most ordinary clays, as we are,
and glazed with my scribbles,
childlike, pure, and blue. After this
you will have to imagine.

2.

Akhmatova writes about being drunk
with love. I lose my breath
in the supermarket when the flesh remembers.
I wouldn't say drunk. Then what
is the word for the lurching step and heart,
the glass reached for and missed?

3.

I watched him pull his belt and buckle it,
fingers moving with the mindless grace of mouths.

"Are words bits of glass?" Richard Hugo asks,
"On a lover's clothes?" On his skin.
I would pick them off with my tongue.

4.

When for whatever reason the man you love
cannot love you, press the pads of your fingers
onto the spill of sesame seeds as they fall
from your bread. Concentrate.

5.

This is not the white sift of domestic filler,
flour or sugar. This is immeasurable blue,
sere as the sea. I will be like daylilies,
defiant in the killing heat of August, searing,
a declaration in winds streaming out of the sun.

Queen Anne's lace shakes her head
in silent recoil when the bee flies away.
                    Pray for rain.

Still, Life

Fishermen at Sea 1796
—J. M. W. Turner

We stand before the one, done when he was twenty,
in which dark night waters circle
a small dory, and there's barely light enough to see.

Tomorrow—if there were one—will be fair. Picture
a squall just ended, the grateful men embracing
calm with deep and slowing breath, a mixture

of exhaustion and relief. At twenty I was marrying, breast
filled with promise, and the night friendly. Aureoles
of whirling light in other galleries do not arrest

the way this canvas does, a simple thing: these men out there alone
the dark more terrifying because permanent, curved
into a bit of painted light, white strokes brightening edges of the
    foam

to a green ordinary as bottles, as familiar.
At the Tate for the first time, I descend to the circular
blond table for coffee. I'm plunged, once there,

into a duplication of design: an Englishwoman tells my life
—it's hers in fact, by chance a replica—to a man, round
eyes sympathetic behind glasses. She's not his wife,

this slender exhibitionist who, as she speaks her secrets, wrings
some sort of pleasure from the public self. I stare into my little disk
of ordinary dark and tell myself I'm safe; I remember everything

I've ever heard about English reserve, but she is louder and more
    graphic
—and less proud—than I could ever be. I lay my spoon beside the
    cup
and rise to leave, as if that's possible. As if the traffic

back and forth to Hell doesn't keep on going on, as if it's possible
  to disembark,
to heave into another life in this quick compass
of the light, this smear of silver brilliance on the vast encircling
  dark.

View from a Thousand Miles Out

Clouds like continents afloat on seas, our lives nets
flung over the curved world and snagged there, events
bright markers at the junctures. Necessary as sin
you walked into the ordinary room that was my life
as one night you would drive your little car
across the path of a fully-loaded tanker and spin
into absolute dark. I have searched the skies
for you with whom those nights I was a girl
again, unfettered. As if memory were mass
and color like the shapes in mouth-blown glass
and could be turned like fragile objects in the hand,
times we were together blend and furl
blur. The moving sky's more permanent than land.
I didn't need you in my arms. I needed you in the world.

Visit, Glasgow School of Art

The Library reaches up like a stave church
and the light is the color of the air in Norway.

Books say it's meant to echo
medieval Scottish castle architecture

but what do books know of the sacred,
how it runs down generations like a river

bearing living brilliance, how it blesses even those
who haven't known the predecessor buildings?

Without design it seems I've brought along
a friend, a painter who has died, to walk

the halls and galleries with me. He observes
the stairwell's tortured tree without comment.

We climb. His presence celebrates the space:
inventive, useful, sacred, bright.

At the top of the steps in streams of clear sky light,
cast and brought from Chartres, *Ancestors of Christ*

prefigures Calvin. He strides through crowds
of youngsters' work nodding his approval and delight.

Outside he'll fade in summer sun but here
in the light from tall windows he flourishes, stops

to admire an ornament, grins fraternally at Mackintosh
and waves a broad salute before he wanders off.

Female Figure in Glass with Copper Wire (6" x 6")

Girdled by copper filament stopped
by knots and twists like miniature barbed
or baling wire, a green glass block

gleams before a three-way mirror in a gallery,
replication of a replication: a little woman
made of metal stands inside. The glass

looks plump and cushiony as if the wire
had been applied before the mass
were cooled, as if the strands were pressed,

not into icy soft-green glass, but flesh.
She does not suffer her imprisonment.
The shapely little figure seems content

within her cube of glass. Arms easy at her sides,
gaze lifted to an absent sun, she satisfies.

Giacometti in Edinburgh

—Scottish National Gallery

To come here you walk along the Water of Leith
a narrow strip of glitter weaving through the wood

like thread through medieval tapestry: burdock
nettle, yarrow, campion and blue forget-me-not

reach for sun through canopies of gold-soaked green.
Dark pools shine with stony constancy and houses lean

over the Water as if Leith were Lethe
and it were possible to see across the narrow stream

to where a meadow opens wide and friendly
as a harbor, strands of tiny brilliant flowers

snagging feet, the hum of bees. All along you know
it isn't only Edinburgh, but your imagination

which folds, repeats, pleats time, and without mass
remembers even places you have never been.

Bank to bank, axon to dendrite, arcs leap
the little space. Beguiled by splendor you begin to see

you've thought—or by not thinking thought—
you could avoid the journey to the banks of that dark stream,

that Charon won't be waiting, and that you'll be ready.
You climb tier after tier of stone steps

cut into the hills and come, short of breath,
to the scowling brow of the museum, stroll

the galleries, find Kline in Giacometti's stroke
and line, fill in the spaces left by figures

who've diminished and then disappeared,
life's warp and weft. Outside, the greensward

plush beneath the wild high Scottish sky
bluer here than elsewhere and benign

for a little time in summer. Taxis squat dark gleams
in sun. An old woman, her arms full of flowers.

Couples holding hands. You will have to give it up, all this:
light tangled in the branches and beneath the trees

in little coins, surprise and hope and grief
and error, and for one brief moment all of it

is glorious. As if King Midas had been waiting
in the woods, stepped out onto the green,

struck everything to polished stillness—
even you, fixed by light, unable to breathe.

Fields Beyond Rosewell

(the accent falls on the second syllable: Rose-well)

Heat rises from the wide resplendent fields
that fall to deep braes, and cattle big and bothies,
sides heaving, lie on the long grass, pink tongues

streaked green from their permanent eating.
I hadn't known I'd needed this, to walk in Europe
and find poppies blazing in their home fields

as if the sun had shrugged his coat of flagrant silk
and fragments of it fell and snagged like flags
on grass and bracken. Bees and mayflies

draw their mad designs on air. It is enough to look.
Above restless greens, the raw uncivil calls of rooks
like fluent echoes of the poppies, and I'm a denim dot

if seen from air, small temporary shadow
crossing fields where broom and mallow
shiver in the wind. Burning nettles, which I fail

to recognize, and nearby analgesic leaves of dock.
At the horizon, cultivated spans of green, flax
before it flowers blue, and swaths of rape—not

gold of gorse like ancient jewelry, but yellow
wild as the hair of girls before life quiets them.
I walk the gravel path along the railroad track

to Rosewell's curving high street in the sun. A lone
old woman watering her shrubs calls out, Scots "o"
deep as loam, Luvvely day! I laugh and call

Indeed it is! Where are the girls parading
babies in their prams, boys tossing balls
and shouting? The men have left because the jobs

have. A few old women tend wee plots
with one rosebush, a foxglove and a hollyhock
walled in by low dark stone before the rows

of shutterless stone houses. Their textures echo
stubble of cut fields, that vacant flatness after harvest.
Houses lean against the empty streets as if they hope

for company, and in the fields nearby, allium
and yarrow tangle in the long wet slick high grasses,
streams grind stone to sand, and in a sky as wide

as anyone has ever needed, clouds contend
like silver at the boil, sweeping over hills
as if a hand had passed across the sun, and lifted.

Villages aren't visible from here, where shadow
chases light across the hills and glen
and fills the crucibles we call our lives,

each poppy-petal wrinkled like burned silk and dead
within the hour. All salvation's now, in steep
unstinting fields. We pick them anyhow.

Lustmord (Retrospective: New York School)

Jenny Holzer exhibit, Barbara Gladstone Gallery,
New York, May 1994

All the tiny bones
lie in rows on the table,
large ones shut
in silver bracelets.

> *I am*
> *awake in*
> *the place*
> *where women die*

You would have to pick them up
to be able to read the words
on the bracelets. I do not pick them up.

> *You confuse me*
> *with something*
> *that is in you*

> *I will not*
> *predict how*
> *you want to*
> *use me*

A group, dress and voices bright
as birds from other hemispheres,
follows a tour-guide, driving me away
from where an electronic sign,
LEDs of red redoubled
in a mirror, reports
sexual violence against women.

On a lower level it is quiet. The table with bones
spreads out like a body scrubbed of blood

and smells and death. The tour-guide says
"They're women's bones."

[S]even women pick at the bones.
I stand in shadow at the corner, write it down.

Bones are mostly inorganic salts.
These appear to be phalanges, metacarpals.
When my mother died we spilled the shards
of her bones under a tree. They clinked
and chunked like broken china.

"The artist's mother was dying." I go
outdoors. A sunny day. In my breast
—is this where memory resides?—the gesture
as a man moves toward me,
whether welcome or a threat read easily.

It is a beautiful day. I sit at a sidewalk cafe
on the corner of West Broadway
and Spring, thinking about the tightrope
that is love and the narrow swinging platform
where the walker rests. Down Spring
near the river is the studio of a man
I once loved. Today I'm remembering
someone else, similar body-type and beard, crush
of his arms around me, southern accents
from the circus town where I was young.
You confuse me Two incredibly handsome men
I will not predict how you want to use me
link arms and head downtown.

The pressure of his arms and chest
took my breath. Erotic
I am awake in the place where
you want to use me
it was quite enough to kill me.

I eat my salad and eggs Benedict
considering Frank O'Hara
and wishing I could paint.

A tour-bus, British Airways logo
on its side, slows as it goes by.
People on the bus take pictures: interesting
Americans eating out of doors.
In my pocket new pounds sterling
for my trip next week. And sure enough,

a week later I'm eating outside at The Swan
across from the Church of St. George the Martyr
watching Brits go by in couples and alone.
It's a gorgeous English summer night, and easy
to imagine I know some things
about the skinny couple in their sixties;
I expect the posing of the young
will lead to bed—*I am awake
in the place where women die*
—where all things end in any case.

I walk across the Thames
on the Waterloo Bridge, rocked
by the memory of his embrace,
the power in his arms to move me, ride
red double-decker buses to the Tate,
stroll the Embankment
in bright sun. Had you seen me,
you'd have seen a woman, blond
and pretty for her fifties, walking.
She'd be cataloguing men
she's loved and men she's tried with,
each a brief suspension
made of light, like a trapeze
in the lowering dark.
You'd observe her long brisk strides
and she'd seem happy, as perhaps she is.

All italicized language is Holzer's.

Acknowledgments

With gratitude to Hawthornden Castle International Retreat for Writers outside Edinburgh where, during a Fellowship in 1996, many of the poems set on mainland Scotland and the islands were begun. Ongoing appreciation to Hawthornden, and to Yaddo, for residencies in the 80's which remain immeasurably important.

Thanks beyond words to Molly Peacock for her many gifts, among them kindness, wisdom.

To Chet Frederick, most special thanks for his unstinting generosity.
To Chris Owen, gratitude for her acuity and heart.
To Bill Holinger, appreciation for his sustaining confidence, and
To Carol Nolde, an early and important reader, warm appreciation.

Over the years, support from Don Hall has been inestimably important; it is a pleasure to express my great thanks to him. I thank also Alicia Ostriker and Jerry Stern; Tom Benediktsson, George Petty, and Kay Tallant, early and helpful readers, and my colleague Carole Stone.

To Sharon Lewis, for heart and mind: thank you.

And to the memory of Richard Hugo, who first showed me Skye.

The author wishes to thank the editors of magazines where some of these poems, often in slightly different form, first appeared.

Faultline: "Lustmord" as "Iconographies (Retrospective, New York School");
Kalliope: "Atlantic Beach," "Satellite Photo";
Lake Effect: "Still, Life";
The Missouri Review: "Mary Clare Writes to Us from Uist, 1730," "Alma Rose Writes to Us from Uist, 1884," "Mary Angela Rose Writes from St Kilda, 1903," "Barbara Rose Writes from South Uist, 1943," "Mairi MacIntyre Writes from St Kilda, 1994," "Mairi's Journal, 8 August," "Mairi MacIntyre Writes to us

from St Kilda, 1994." "[You Go Back]," "Mairi's Journal—
August," "Eventually They Come Ashore";
*Phoebe: An Interdisciplinary Journal of Feminist Scholarship,
Theory, and Aesthetics*: "The Natural Element";
The Studio Potter : "Kiln";
Southern Lights / PEN South: "Migrations";
Two Rivers Review: "Mostly Sky" as "Another Woman's Husband",
"Starshine."

* * *

Books which were important adjuncts to what I learned in Scotland
include *Thatched Houses of the Old Highlands*, by Colin Sinclair;
St Kilda, the Continuing Story of the Islands, ed. Meg Buchanan;
Last Greetings from St Kilda, by Bob Charnley, and *St Kilda*, by
David Quine (in the Colin Baxter Island Guides Series). Mention
must also be made of the wonderful Museum of Island Life outside
Kilmuir on Skye where I saw photographs and objects from island
homes. Thanks to Tom Ihde and Kara Smith for consultations on
Scots and Gaelic.

With thanks to Montclair State University for its Faculty Scholar-
ship Incentive Program which provided time to work, and

Special appreciation to Steve Huff, Sarah Freligh, and Thom Ward—
the community at BOA.

About the Author

Deena Linett lives in Montclair, New Jersey, from whose hills it is possible to see the towers of New York. She teaches at Montclair State University and has won national contests for the novels *On Common Ground*, and *The Translator's Wife*, as well as for short fiction. Twice a Yaddo Fellow, she has also been resident at Hawthornden Castle International Retreat for Writers in Scotland. The mother of three children, she dedicates this book to twin granddaughters who someday will be able to read it.

BOA EDITIONS, LTD.

THE A. POULIN, JR. NEW POETS OF AMERICA SERIES